To my bear Sam
—L.P.

For Tasha and Miika Greenwood

Special thanks to Teddy Bear collectors
Laura Hart, Jill McDonald, and Amy Wheeler,
and also to Mrs. Wheeler's 3rd grade class
—J.W.

http://www.randomhouse.com/

Library of Congress Cataloging-in-Publication Data
Penner, Lucille Recht. The teddy bear book / written by Lucille Recht Penner ;
illustrated by Jody Wheeler.
p. cm. Summary: Contains a variety of projects with a teddy bear theme, including
making stuffed bears, decorated tee shirts, puppets, jewelry, party foods, and more.
ISBN 0-679-88091-7 (trade)
1. Soft toy making—Juvenile literature. 2. Teddy bears—Juvenile literature.
3. Handicraft—Juvenile literature. 4. Cookery—Juvenile literature.
[1. Teddy bears. 2. Handicraft.] I. Wheeler, Jody, ill. II. Title.
TT174.3.P46 1997 745.592'4—dc20 96-2645

Printed in the United States of America

10 9 8 7 6 5 4 3 2 1

The Teddy Bear Book

by LUCILLE RECHT PENNER
illustrated by JODY WHEELER

Random House New York

CONTENTS

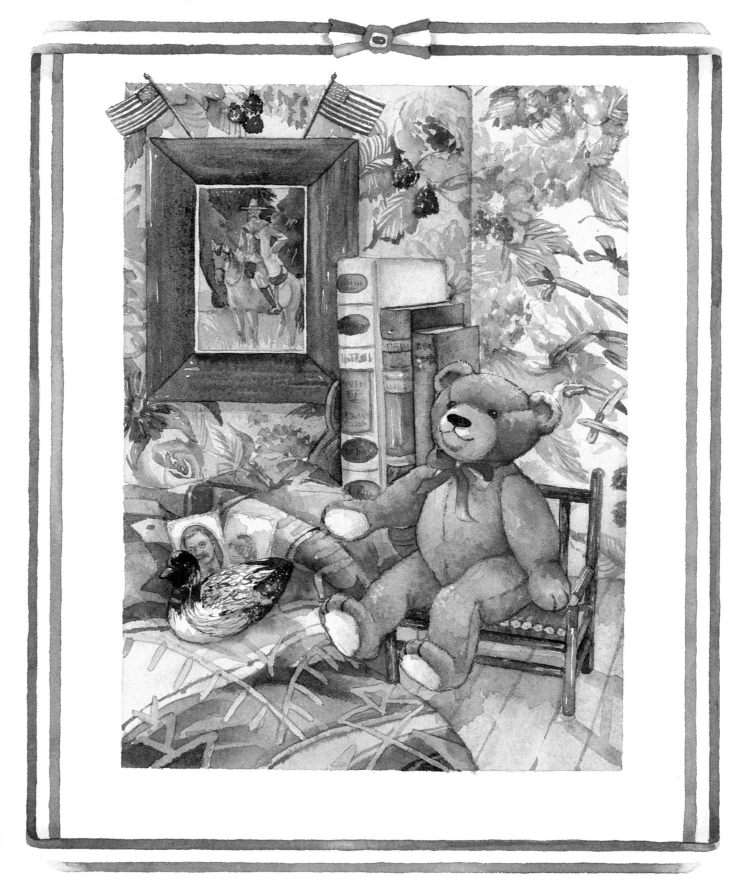

The First Teddy Bear

Teddy Bears are soft, cuddly, and lots of fun. But where do they come from? Who made the first one? No one knows for sure.

The first little stuffed bear may have been made in honor of the 26th president of the United States—Teddy Roosevelt.

One day, President Roosevelt went on a hunting trip. What was he hunting? Bear! But he couldn't find any. So his friends found a little bear cub for him and tied it to a tree. "Go ahead," they said. "Shoot."

"No!" Teddy said. "If I shoot that little bear, I can never look my children in the eye again."

The story about President Teddy Roosevelt and the bear cub was printed in all the newspapers. A shopkeeper who read it made a little stuffed bear and called it *Teddy's Bear*. He sold it right away and made more.

The stuffed bears were a huge success! Everyone wanted one. Teddy Bears became one of the most popular toys in the world.

Do *you* love Teddy Bears?

If you do, then this book is the perfect companion for you. It's full of delightful ideas for growing a Teddy Bear Garden, throwing a Bear Day Party, making a stunning wardrobe of Teddy Bear T-shirts, tucking your bear in at night with a lovely quilt that you design yourself, and creating lots of cuddly and charming Teddies.

Make all the Teddy Bears in this book and then think of your own ideas. Your imagination will grow along with your Teddy collection. Welcome to the wonderful world of Teddy Bears!

Stuffed Teddy Bears

Teddy Bear, Teddy Bear,
I love you.

A SOFT TEDDY
SCENTED SACHET TEDDY BEARS
TEDDY BEAR BEANBAG TOY
HOLIDAY BEARS

What's the softest, sweetest toy you ever had? Is it a Teddy Bear? Teddies are lots of fun. They like being dressed up and playing games. And you can tell your Teddy anything. Teddy will always keep your secrets.

It's fun to make your own Teddy Bears. And it's easy. You can make big ones and little ones, soft, huggy ones and sweet, scented ones.

After all, you can never have too many Teddy Bears!

A SOFT TEDDY

You will need:	*a big piece of paper*	*soft flannel fabric*
pins	*needle and thread*	*polyester filling*
felt	*glue*	*fabric paint or buttons*
ribbon	*scissors*	

Draw a Teddy Bear shape about 12 inches long on a big piece of paper. Cut it out to make a pattern.

Fold the fabric in half. Pin on the pattern and cut around it. You will have two identical Teddy Bear–shaped pieces of fabric. Sew the right sides of the fabric together, but leave a little opening on the inside of one leg. Turn the fabric inside out through the opening and stuff it loosely with polyester filling. Sew up the opening.

Stitch across the top of the arms and legs of the Teddy and the bottom of the ears.

Cut patches out of felt for each of the paws and the muzzle. Glue them onto the Teddy.

Sew on buttons for the eyes and nose or paint them on with fabric paint. Now tie a pretty ribbon around your new Teddy. And give it a hug!

SCENTED SACHET TEDDY BEARS

You will need:

a piece of paper	*flowered fabric*	*pins*
needle and thread	*dried lavender or rose petals*	*felt*
glue	*buttons or fabric paint*	*ribbon*

Follow the directions for making a Soft Teddy on pages 10–12, but make your pattern only 5 inches long and cut it out of pretty flowered fabric. Stuff your little bear with crumbled dried lavender or rose petals.

Put scented sachet Teddies in all your drawers or hang them from a ribbon in your closet. They'll make your clothes smell like flowers.

TEDDY BEAR BEANBAG TOY

You will need:

a piece of paper	*pins*	*lightweight denim or corduroy fabric*
dried beans	*felt*	*needle and thread*
glue	*ribbon*	*buttons or fabric paint*
		scissors

Follow the directions for making a Soft Teddy Bear on pages 10–12, but make your pattern only 8 inches long and cut it out of lightweight denim or corduroy. Stuff it with dried beans.

HOLIDAY BEARS
Christmas! Halloween! Valentine's Day!

Make special Teddy Bears for all your favorite holidays. It's easy. Follow the instructions for making a Soft Teddy on pages 10–12, but cut Holiday Bears out of material printed with colorful holiday designs. Tie a matching ribbon around the bear's neck.

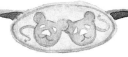

The Teddy Show

A Handful of Bears
Ballerina Bear
Teddy Bear Stage

Teddy Bear puppets are wonderful actors. Especially if you help. You'll enjoy making these puppets and a special theater for them to perform in. When you're finished, you can put on plays you make up yourself, or act out a fairy tale.

A Handful of Bears

You will need:
a piece of paper   *old gloves*
pins   *felt in several colors*   *fabric glue*
needle and thread   *scissors*

Make a handful of Teddy Bear Puppets out of an old glove. You can create a mother, father, two children, and a baby Teddy.

Draw a finger-sized Teddy Bear on a piece of paper. Cut out the pattern, pin it onto the felt, and cut around it. Repeat until you have five Teddy Bears. Glue on scraps of different-colored felt for eyes, noses, mouths, and clothes. Sew the Teddy family onto the glove.

Slip on your puppet glove and bring the Bear Family to life!

BALLERINA BEAR

Do you love the ballet? Make an elegant Ballerina Bear.

You will need:
construction paper   satin ribbon (¼ inch wide)   markers
double-sided tape   glue   scissors

On a piece of construction paper, draw a small Teddy Bear about 3 inches long wearing a ballerina skirt. Don't draw its legs. Your fingers will be the legs. Cut out two circles about ½ inch apart to put your fingers through.

Color the ballerina's face and blouse with markers. Then cut little paws out of construction paper.

Now make a satin skirt out of ribbon. Put a strip of glue along the ballerina's waist. Cut 1-inch strips of ribbon and stick the edges onto the glue.

Push two fingers through the holes in your puppet. Tape the paws to the ends of your fingers. Now strike up the music, wiggle your fingers, and dance, ballerina, dance!

TEDDY BEAR STAGE

It's easy to make a beautiful theater you can use over and over again.

You will need:
cardboard carton   *gold and silver stars*   *contact paper*
tablecloth   *Teddy Bear stickers*   *scissors*

Ask an adult to help you cut the flaps off the top of a cardboard carton, then turn it over and cut a rectangle out of the bottom.

Cover the outside of the box with strips of contact paper.

Decorate it with Teddy Bear stickers and gold and silver stars.

Drape a long tablecloth over a table. Put your theater on top of the table and crouch behind it. The tablecloth will hide you from the audience. Hold up your puppets and move them around to act out a story. It's showtime!

17

Sweet Teddies

Mother dear,
I sadly fear
My appetite
Is always here.

CHOCOLATE BABY BEARS
BUTTON BEARS
CUBCAKES

CHOCOLATE BABY BEARS

You will need:
vanilla wafers   *gumdrops*   *peanut butter*
chocolate icing   *chocolate chips*   *small candies*
chocolate sprinkles   *raisins*

It's fun to make delicious Teddy Bear Babies with vanilla wafers, candies, raisins, peanut butter, and icing.

Use the cookies for the head and body. Stick on gumdrop ears, muzzle, and paws with dabs of peanut butter. Cover the bear with chocolate icing. Press on a chocolate chip nose and small candy eyes. Add sprinkles if you want a fuzzy-looking baby bear. Use your imagination to put together other bears with your favorite foods.

BUTTON BEARS

You will need:

7 oz. marzipan

¾ teaspoon vanilla extract

red, green, and yellow food coloring

1 oz. dark or milk chocolate

Divide the marzipan into three equal parts. Knead three drops of one of the food colors and ¼ teaspoon of vanilla extract into each part. Continue kneading until the marzipan is soft and smooth.

Divide each color into four balls for heads and eight smaller balls for ears. Press the ears onto the heads and flatten them.

Ask an adult to melt the chocolate in the top of a double boiler. Remove from the heat. Dip part of each head into the chocolate. Set the Button Bears on a piece of waxed paper to dry. Makes 12 Button Bears.

CUBCAKES

You will need:

scissors

big chocolate cookies

small candies

a piece of paper or cardboard

powdered sugar

peanut butter

Cut Teddy Bear heads out of paper. Put a paper head on each cookie. Sift powdered sugar all over the cookies. Lift the paper heads carefully. You will see brown Teddy Bear heads. Use small candies to decorate the eyes, nose, and mouth on each cookie. Put a dab of peanut butter on each candy so that it will stick to the cookie.

Decorate all the cubcakes, arrange them, and serve at once.

19

The Teddy Gallery

FANCY FRAMES
A TEDDY EGG SCULPTURE
LITTLE STONE BEARS
A FUZZY WUZZY PICTURE

Would you like to create an art gallery in your own room? You can hang up great Teddy Bear pictures in fancy frames and show off your Stone Bears and Teddy sculptures.

FANCY FRAMES

You will need: | *precut mat* | *magazines*
catalogs | *scraps of fabric* | *colored foil*
Teddy Bear stickers | *glue* | *metallic star stickers*
construction paper | *scissors* | *adhesive picture hooks*

Precut mats make great frames. They come in many colors and sizes. Choose your favorite. You'll find them in crafts stores.

Cut Teddy Bears out of magazines, catalogs, construction paper, scraps of fabric, and colored foil. Glue them onto the mat. Add more glamor with Teddy Bear and metallic star stickers.

Paint, draw, or snap a picture of your favorite bear to put in your new frame. Attach an adhesive picture hook to the back of the mat and hang up your beautiful picture.

A TEDDY EGG SCULPTURE

You will need:

felt   small plastic bottle cap   glue

hard-boiled egg   acrylic paint   felt-tipped markers

scissors

Cut a strip of felt to fit around the bottle cap. Glue it in place. Paint the egg. When the paint dries, draw the eyes, nose, and mouth with markers.

Cut ears and two paws out of felt. Glue them onto the egg. Place the felt-covered bottle cap upside down to make a stand for your little round Teddy. Handle it gently. If you don't break the shell, a hard-boiled Teddy Egg sculpture will last for years.

LITTLE STONE BEARS

You will need: smooth, flat stone   acrylic paint

Wash a smooth, flat stone. Put it in the sun until it's completely dry. Paint it white. Let the paint dry. Paint on another coat of white paint. When it's dry, you are ready to paint your bear. First, draw it lightly in pencil. Then paint in the colors.

A stone Teddy can be any colors you choose. It can even have polka dots. Use your imagination to make it beautiful.

A FUZZY WUZZY PICTURE

Fuzzy Wuzzy was a bear.
Fuzzy Wuzzy had no hair.
Fuzzy Wuzzy wasn't fuzzy,
Was he?

You will need:
precut rug yarn
ribbon

posterboard
glue-on movable doll's eyes
adhesive picture hook

glue
button
scissors

Draw an outline of a Teddy Bear on a piece of posterboard. Cut it out. Spread a thin layer of glue on each foot. Press on strands of precut yarn. Cover small areas above the feet with glue and yarn. It's okay if some of the yarn overlaps.

Continue adding yarn until the entire Teddy Bear is covered.

Cut little holes in the yarn for the movable doll's eyes and a button nose. Glue them on. Tie a ribbon around the Teddy's neck.

When the glue dries, turn the Teddy Bear over. Glue an adhesive picture hook on the back.

Hang your Fuzzy Wuzzy Teddy Bear on the wall and stand back. Fuzzy Wuzzy's *very* fuzzy, indeed!

Teddy Tees

I ♥ My Teddy Bear
A Teddy Puff
Sequins and Sparkles
Teddies and Bows

You can't always have your Teddy Bear with you. Teddies don't usually go to school or to dinner at a fancy restaurant. So do the next best thing. Wear a gorgeous Teddy Bear T-shirt when you step out. They're fun to make.

I ♥ My Teddy Bear

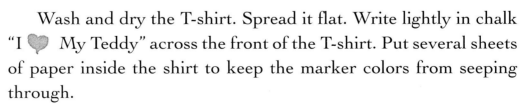

You will need:

white cotton T-shirt   *colored chalk*
several sheets of paper   *fabric marker*

Wash and dry the T-shirt. Spread it flat. Write lightly in chalk "I ♥ My Teddy" across the front of the T-shirt. Put several sheets of paper inside the shirt to keep the marker colors from seeping through.

Write over the chalk marks with your favorite color fabric marker. Fill in the heart with red marker. This T-shirt will have a special place in your heart.

A TEDDY PUFF

You will need:

white cotton T-shirt　　　　*chalk*
several sheets of paper　　　*bead paint*

Wash and dry the T-shirt. Spread it flat. Draw a Teddy Bear with chalk. Put several sheets of paper inside the shirt to keep the paint from seeping through.

Now paint the Teddy by squeezing dots of paint directly from the tube along the chalk marks. As the paint dries, the dots will puff up and look like little beads.

SEQUINS AND SPARKLES

You will need:

chalk　　　　　　　　　　　　*white cotton T-shirt*
glue-on movable doll's eyes　*iron-on sequin ribbons*
fake jewels　　　　　　　　　*fabric glue*
　　　　　　　　　　　　　　　fabric markers

Wash and dry the T-shirt. Spread it flat. Draw an outline of a Teddy Bear in chalk. Pin sequin ribbons in place around the outline. Ask an adult to help you iron the shirt according to the instructions on the sequin ribbons.

Now decorate the Teddy. Glue on the movable doll's eyes and fake jewels for the paws and ears. Draw the nose and mouth with fabric marker. You'll be able to go anywhere in this elegant tee.

TEDDIES AND BOWS

You will need:

white T-shirt	*several sheets of paper*	*potato*
fabric paint	*¼-inch-wide satin ribbon*	*knife*

Wash and dry the T-shirt. Spread it flat. Put several sheets of paper inside the shirt to keep the paint from seeping through.

Cut the potato in half. Draw a Teddy Bear on it with a pencil. Ask an adult to help you cut away the potato so the Teddy stands out.

Brush paint onto the raised Teddy shape. Press it onto your T-shirt. Pull the potato off carefully. Paint the shape again and press it on another spot. Keep on painting and printing until you have little Teddy Bears all over your shirt.

While the paint dries, make little bows out of the satin ribbon. Sew one on each Teddy Bear.

If you make a lot of Teddy Tees, you can have a fashion parade. Invite a photographer and guests who love clothes.

Teddy Books

TEDDY BEAR STORYBOOK
ZIGZAG NAME BOOK
A PEEPHOLE BEAR BOOK

Read to your Teddy Bear every day. And if you really want to surprise him, make some of your own books—Teddy Bear books—just for him.

TEDDY BEAR STORYBOOK

You will need:

4 sheets of 8 x 11-inch paper	*stapler*	*pencil*
scissors	*markers or crayons*	*pen*

Put the sheets of paper in a neat stack. Fold the stack in half lengthwise. It will look like a little book. Staple along the folded edge. Draw a Teddy Bear lightly in pencil on the top page. This will be the cover of your book. Cut around the outline of the bear. Make sure you don't cut off all the staples. Color the cover with markers or crayons.

Now write your story in the book with a pen. Draw pictures with markers or crayons.

Write the title of the book and your own name on the cover. You are the author!

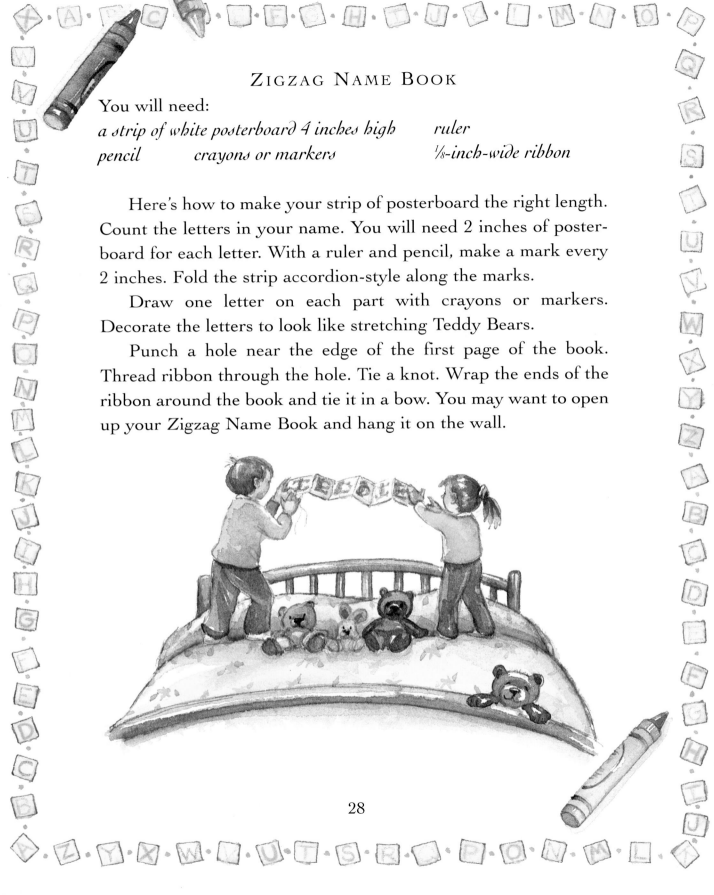

ZIGZAG NAME BOOK

You will need:

a strip of white posterboard 4 inches high   ruler

pencil   crayons or markers   ⅛-inch-wide ribbon

Here's how to make your strip of posterboard the right length. Count the letters in your name. You will need 2 inches of posterboard for each letter. With a ruler and pencil, make a mark every 2 inches. Fold the strip accordion-style along the marks.

Draw one letter on each part with crayons or markers. Decorate the letters to look like stretching Teddy Bears.

Punch a hole near the edge of the first page of the book. Thread ribbon through the hole. Tie a knot. Wrap the ends of the ribbon around the book and tie it in a bow. You may want to open up your Zigzag Name Book and hang it on the wall.

A PEEPHOLE BEAR BOOK

You will need:

6 sheets of 4 x 6-inch paper   *scissors*   *stapler*
crayons or markers   *felt*   *glue*

Stack five sheets of paper. Draw a 2-inch circle in the middle of the top sheet. Fold the stack lightly and cut out the circle. Unfold the stack. You now have five pieces of paper with a hole in the middle. Put them on top of the sixth sheet of paper. Staple all the sheets together along one long edge.

Draw a Teddy Bear head in the middle of the circle. Cut out a small, round piece of felt and glue it over the Teddy's nose.

Write A PEEPHOLE BEAR BOOK over the peephole on the first page. Below the peephole, write the name of the author: You.

Now turn to the first page. You can see the Teddy Bear's head through the peephole. With crayons or markers, draw its body doing something. Playing basketball? Eating an ice cream cone? Standing on its head? Turn the pages. Draw the Teddy Bear doing something different on each page. On the last page show the Teddy Bear waving good-bye.

The Teddy Bears' Picnic

Today's the day the Teddy Bears have their picnic.
Every Teddy Bear who's been good is sure of a treat today.
There are lots of marvelous things to eat.
And wonderful games to play.

PEANUT BUTTER AND HONEY BEARS
TEDDY BEAR CRUNCHES
CHEESE PAWS
READY, TEDDY!

Has your Teddy Bear been good? Take him on a special picnic. Bring along all the foods Teddy Bears love best. And play games a Teddy can join in.

PEANUT BUTTER AND HONEY BEARS

You will need:
sliced brown bread   *bear-shaped cookie cutter*
peanut butter   *honey*

Cut an even number of bear shapes out of sliced bread with your cookie cutter. Spread half of them with peanut butter. Spread the rest of them with honey. Carefully put the honey shapes over the peanut butter shapes. Make lots of these sandwiches. Even people love them.

TEDDY BEAR CRUNCHES

Teddy Bear Crunches are healthy and fun to munch on.

You will need:
¼ cup raisins   *¼ cup roasted peanuts, shelled*
⅛ cup sunflower seeds   *½ cup granola*
four 4-inch squares of silver foil   *Teddy Bear stickers*

Mix the raisins, peanuts, sunflower seeds, and granola together.

Spread out the squares of silver foil. Heap one quarter of the mixture in the middle of each square. Fold the ends over to make a bundle. Seal it with a Teddy Bear sticker.

CHEESE PAWS

You will need:
piece of white paper   *4 oz. butter*   *1 cup flour*
½ cup grated cheese   *ice water (about 3 tbs.)*
rolling pin   *sesame seeds*   *a knife*

Draw a bear's paw about 3 inches long on a piece of white paper. Cut it out.

Ask an adult to preheat the oven to 350°.

Cut the butter into small pieces. Put it in a bowl with the flour. Use your fingertips to mash them together until the mixture looks like bread crumbs. Stir in the grated cheese. Add ice water, a few drops at a time, until the mixture forms a soft dough.

Roll out the dough with a rolling pin on a floured surface. Put the bear pattern on top and cut around it. Cut out as many paws as you can and put them on a buttered cookie sheet. Gather up the scraps of dough and roll them out again to make more paws.

Sprinkle the paws with sesame seeds. Ask an adult to put them in the oven. Bake until they are golden, 10–12 minutes. Makes 24 Cheese Paws.

READY, TEDDY!

You will need:
2 Teddy Bears

Divide your friends into two teams. Have each team form a line. Tuck a Teddy under the chin of the first person in each line.

Then shout, "Ready, Teddy!"

Teammates must pass their Teddy down the line without using their hands. If their Teddy falls on the ground, they have to start all over again from the beginning.

The first team to get its Teddy to the end wins.

The Teddy Bear Garden

How does your garden grow?

Do you and your Teddy Bear have green thumbs? Plant a garden near a sunny window.

What will you grow there? Teddy Bears, of course!

GROW A TEDDY BEAR

You will need: *basil, watercress, or parsley seeds*
small, flat sponge   *spray bottle*   *scissors*

Cut a Teddy Bear shape out of the sponge. Dip the sponge in water and wring it out. Put it on a flat plate on a sunny windowsill. Sprinkle the sponge with seeds.

Fill the spray bottle with water. Spray the sponge every day to keep it wet. Soon your Teddy will grow a green coat.

34

FLOWERPOT FACES

You will need:
terra-cotta flowerpots   *acrylic paint*

It's fun to grow plants in lovely flowerpots that you decorate yourself. Paint happy Teddy faces on each pot. Use bright colors.

When the paint dries, fill the pots with planting soil and healthy green plants. Water them well, and put them in a sunny spot.

PLANT A PICTURE BEAR

You will need: *magazines and catalogs*
small sticks   *cardboard*   *tape*
glue   *flowerpot filled with soil* *scissors*

Cut pictures of Teddy Bears out of magazines or catalogs. Glue them onto a piece of cardboard. Cut around them.

Tape the pictures onto small sticks and "plant" them in a flower-pot filled with soil. It's also nice to plant a Picture Bear in a pot with a real plant in it.

A GARDEN PARTY

When you finish making your Teddy Bear Garden, have a garden party. Invite your friends and family to admire your special garden. Give them each a Picture Bear to plant.

Happy Bear Day

*My love for you
Will never fail,
As long as Teddy
Has a tail.*

A TEDDY BEAR BIRTHDAY CAKE
POLAR BEAR PUNCH
A BEAR DAY BANNER
WHO LOVES TEDDY?

If you and your Teddy Bear like a good party, celebrate Bear Day. When is Bear Day? Whenever you like!

A TEDDY BEAR BIRTHDAY CAKE

You will need:

chocolate icing

chocolate-covered creams

small round or heart-shaped candies

a chocolate sheet cake

chocolate sprinkles

black string licorice

a knife

Ask an adult to help you prepare a chocolate sheet cake using a 9 x 13-inch baking pan. After the cake cools, cut out a Teddy Bear shape. Cover it with chocolate icing. Before the icing sets, cover the cake with chocolate sprinkles to look like fur. Put chocolate-covered creams in place for the Teddy's eyes and nose. Use string licorice for its mouth. Make a pattern of polka dots or hearts with small candies. Happy Bear Day!

POLAR BEAR PUNCH

Polar Bear Punch is easy to make and very refreshing. Serve it in a tall, clear glass.

You will need: *vanilla ice cream*
milk *cream soda*

Put ¼ cup milk in each glass. Add a scoop of vanilla ice cream. Fill the glass with sparkling cream soda.

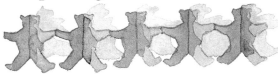

A BEAR DAY BANNER

You will need:
construction paper *¼-inch-wide ribbon (four 12-inch lengths)*
markers *tape* *scissors*

Cut two pieces of construction paper in half lengthwise. Fold each piece, accordion-style, into eight sections. Draw a Teddy Bear on each one. The middle of the bear's body and each of its paws should be on the folds. Cut out the bears, without cutting through the folds. Open up the papers and draw eyes, nose, and mouth on each bear.

Tape the paper bears together. Write *HAPPY BEAR DAY* on them. Put one letter on each bear, but draw a star on the first and last bear and the two bears that mark the spaces between words. Use different colored markers for each letter.

Tie each piece of ribbon in a bow. Curl the ends. Tape the bow onto each star so the ends hang down. Hang the banner over the party table. When the party's over, put it away carefully. You can use it again when Bear Day comes around again.

WHO LOVES TEDDY?

You will need: *large piece of paper*   *red construction paper*
marker   *double-sided tape*   *scissors*

With a marker, draw a Teddy Bear on a large piece of paper.

Cut hearts out of red construction paper. Make enough for each player, with one left over. Tape the extra heart on the paper Teddy. Put a piece of tape on each of the other hearts.

Tape the paper Teddy to a tree. Make sure there are no low branches that a guest could walk into!

Give each player a heart. When it's her turn, blindfold her, turn her around twice, and point her toward the tree. Whoever sticks her heart closest to the heart on the paper Teddy is the winner.

Gorgeous Teddy Bear Jewelry

BEADS AND BEARS
TEDDY BEAR CHARMS
SILVER TEDDY PIN

Do you like to get dressed up? You'll look glamorous in this gorgeous Teddy Bear jewelry that you make yourself.

BEADS AND BEARS

You will need:
pastel pink yarn
pink fake jewel

¼-inch-wide white satin ribbon
pink posterboard
bead

glue
scissors

Make a stunning necklace out of satin ribbon, yarn, a bead, and a little bear.

First make the chain for your necklace by braiding together one piece of satin ribbon and two pieces of yarn.

Cut a 2-inch bear out of posterboard. Ask an adult to help you punch a hole in the top of the bear's head. Cut a small piece of ribbon. Tie a bow in the center. Glue the ribbon on the Teddy Bear's neck to make a bow tie. When the glue dries, trim the edges. Glue the pink fake jewel below the bow tie.

Tie a fat knot in the middle of the ribbon and yarn chain. Thread the two ends of the chain through the hole in the Teddy Bear. Then thread them through the bead.

Put the necklace around your neck and tie the ends of the chain together.

TEDDY BEAR CHARMS

You will need:
¼ cup water
¼ cup salt

food coloring (about 10 drops)
½ cup flour
1 teaspoon corn oil

It's easy to make Teddy Bear charms out of colored play dough.

Mix food coloring and water to make your favorite color.

Stir together flour and salt. Stir in the oil and colored water. Knead the dough until it's soft and smooth. Shape small pieces of dough into Teddy Bear charms.

Ask an adult to preheat the oven to 325°.

Make a small hole in the top of each charm with a toothpick. Place the charms on a cookie sheet and bake 40 minutes. Cool. Add the charm to your favorite charm bracelet. You'll have enough dough to make extra charms for your friends.

SILVER TEDDY PIN

You will need:
glue
safety pin

posterboard
fake jewels
tape

silver foil
felt
scissors

Cut a 2-inch Teddy Bear out of posterboard. Cover it with silver foil. Glue on fake jewels for the eyes and bits of felt for the nose and tail. Turn the Teddy over and tape a safety pin on the other side.

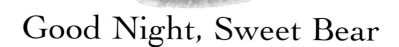

Good Night, Sweet Bear

Teddy Bear, Teddy Bear,
Turn out the light.
Teddy Bear, Teddy Bear,
Say good night.

BEARS, RIBBONS, AND HEARTS PILLOW
SWEET TEDDY BEAR QUILT
GOOD NIGHTCAP

It's time to go to sleep. Make sure your Teddy Bear is tucked in with a beautiful pillow, quilt, and nightcap.

BEARS, RIBBONS, AND HEARTS PILLOW

You will need:
small solid-colored polyester throw pillow
chalk
fabric paint
½-inch-wide ribbon (four 8-inch lengths)

Draw a sleeping Teddy Bear head on one side of the pillow with chalk. Paint the Teddy with fabric paint. Paint little red hearts in each corner.

Tie each piece of ribbon in a bow and sew one bow on each of the hearts.

SWEET TEDDY BEAR QUILT

You will need:
36-inch square of double-sided quilted material
chalk
fabric paint
½-inch-wide ribbon (four 8-inch lengths)

Hem the edges of the quilted material. Spread it out on a flat surface. Draw sleeping Teddy Bears with chalk. Paint the bears with fabric paint.

If you want the quilt to match your pillow, paint little red hearts in the corners. Tie each piece of ribbon in a bow and sew one bow on each of the hearts.

GOOD NIGHTCAP

Your Teddy Bear will enjoy wearing a nightcap to sleep. It's warm and very pretty.

You will need: *ruler*   *paper*
pencil   *fabric*   *chalk*
yarn   *yarn needle*   *scissors*

Measure your Teddy Bear's head. Draw a circle 2 inches wider on a piece of paper. Then draw another circle 8 inches wider on another piece of paper. Cut out the circles.

Pin the big paper circle on a piece of fabric and cut around it. Put the small paper circle in the middle of the fabric circle and draw a line around it with chalk.

Thread a long piece of yarn on a yarn needle and sew around the chalk circle with running stitches.

Pull up the yarn from each end to gather the material slightly. Tie the ends in a bow.

Sweet dreams, Teddy Bear.